To Dempssey
Love
Grandma meme 2004

LEMUR Landing

A Story of a Madagascan Tropical Dry Forest

by Deborah Dennard

Illustrated by Kristin Kest

For Katy, Amanda, and Kelly—D.D.

To my Buddy, Mark, with possumly love—K^2

Book layout: Marcin D. Pilchowski
Editor: Judy Gitenstein
Editorial assistance: Chelsea Shriver

First edition 2001
10 9 8 7 6 5 4 3 2 1
Printed in China

Acknowledgments:
   Our very special thanks to Dorothy Clark and the staff at the Duke University Primate Center for their curatorial review.
   Additional thanks to Patrick S. Daniels of the Duke University Primate Center and to Rick Hudson, Fort Worth Zoological Park.

Library of Congress Cataloging-in-Publication Data

Dennard, Deborah.
      Lemur landing: a story of a Madagascan tropical dry forest / by Deborah Dennard ; illustrated by Kristin Kest. — 1st ed.
         p. cm.
Summary: In the tropical dry forest of Southern Madagascar, a baby ring-tailed lemur follows his troop through their forest home in search of food and water.
   ISBN 1-56899-978-X (alk. paper) — ISBN 1-56899-979-8 (pbk. : alk. paper)
   1. Ring-tailed lemur—Juvenile fiction. [1. Ring-tailed lemur—Fiction. 2. Lemurs—Fiction. 3. Zoology—Madagascar—Fiction.] I. Kest, Kristin, ill. II. Title.

   PZ10.3.D386 Le 2001
   [E] — dc21

                                                    00-063756

LEMUR Landing

A Story of a Madagascan Tropical Dry Forest

by Deborah Dennard
Illustrated by Kristin Kest

Soundprints
Where Children Discover...

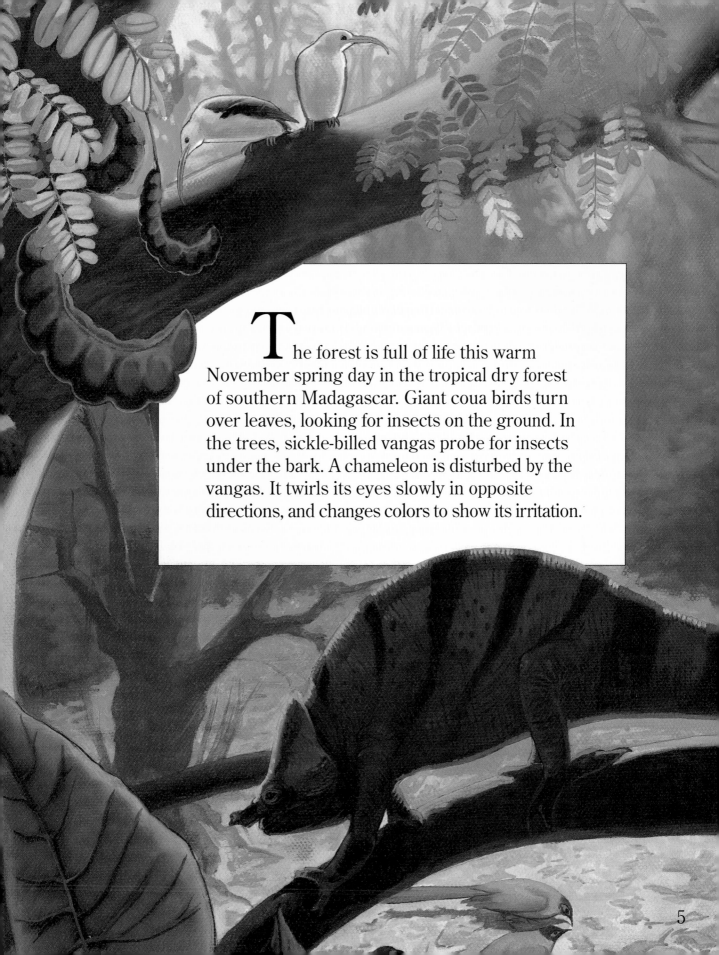

The forest is full of life this warm November spring day in the tropical dry forest of southern Madagascar. Giant coua birds turn over leaves, looking for insects on the ground. In the trees, sickle-billed vangas probe for insects under the bark. A chameleon is disturbed by the vangas. It twirls its eyes slowly in opposite directions, and changes colors to show its irritation.

Fuzzy black-and-white tails dangle in a line from a branch high in a tamarind tree. The tails belong to a troop of ring-tailed lemurs, small primates that look more like cats or squirrels than monkeys. They sit with outstretched arms and legs facing the morning sun, basking in the warmth and the safety of their troop. Eyes closed, the female leader sits with her baby, surrounded by the troop.

Restless with the daily sunbathing routine, the baby ring-tail leaps recklessly from his mother's lap. His arms and legs fly in all directions. He barely manages to grab hold of another lemur's tail. The baby cries out for his mother. Stretching out an arm, she helps him return to her lap, then mews softly to comfort him. Using her bottom comb-like grooming teeth, she cleans her baby from head to tail. Soon the whole troop joins in a flurry of mutual grooming.

The female leader signals the others with clicks and groans. They answer and follow as she springs to the ground. The small troop of seven adults, three babies, plus a pair of year old youngsters follow a well worn path through the forest. Daily they follow the path to find food and water and to keep an eye on the territory they call home. Females with big-eyed babies on their backs lead, and males follow at the rear. Last year's youngsters scamper back and forth, playing as they go. The lemurs walk on all fours, back legs higher than front, tails held up in gracefully swaying curves.

Suddenly a baby screams in alarm at a movement in the grass. The lemurs stop and chatter their concern. The grass parts and out shuffles a radiated tortoise. Yellow stripes spiral out on its high-domed shell. The sight of the tortoise is new and frightening to the baby. The adults know the tortoise poses no threat. As the baby grows, she too will learn. When she is calmed the troop moves on.

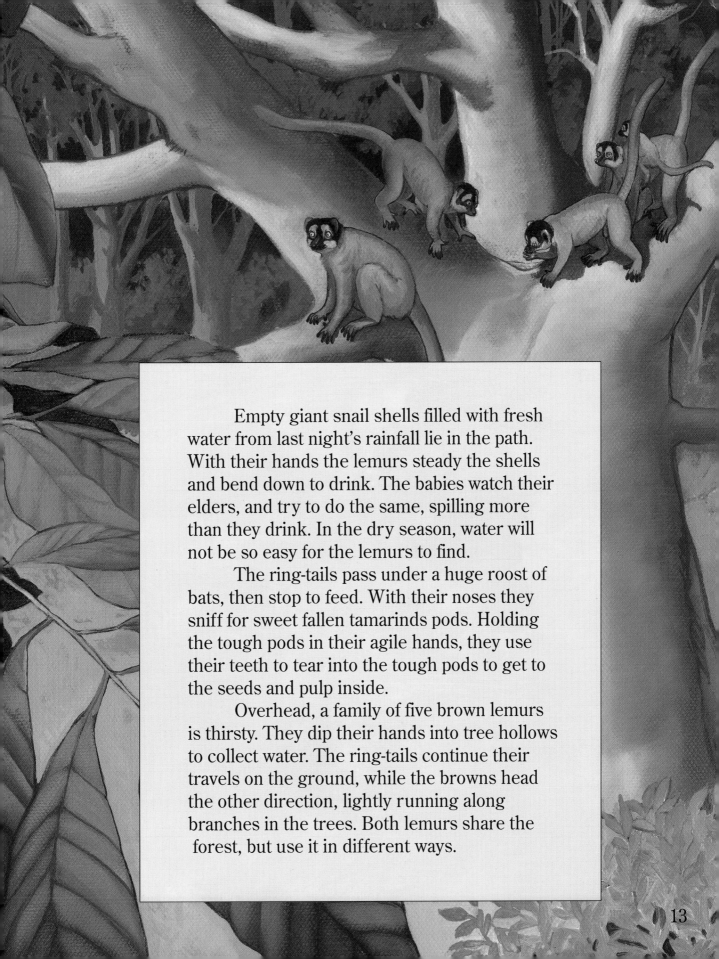

Empty giant snail shells filled with fresh water from last night's rainfall lie in the path. With their hands the lemurs steady the shells and bend down to drink. The babies watch their elders, and try to do the same, spilling more than they drink. In the dry season, water will not be so easy for the lemurs to find.

The ring-tails pass under a huge roost of bats, then stop to feed. With their noses they sniff for sweet fallen tamarinds pods. Holding the tough pods in their agile hands, they use their teeth to tear into the tough pods to get to the seeds and pulp inside.

Overhead, a family of five brown lemurs is thirsty. They dip their hands into tree hollows to collect water. The ring-tails continue their travels on the ground, while the browns head the other direction, lightly running along branches in the trees. Both lemurs share the forest, but use it in different ways.

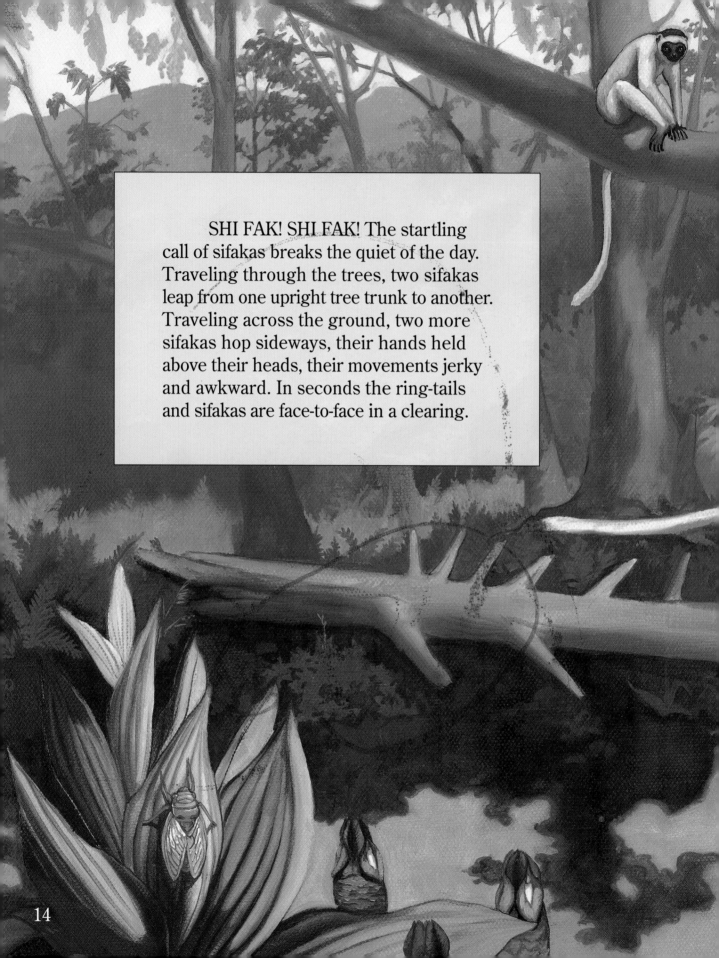

SHI FAK! SHI FAK! The startling call of sifakas breaks the quiet of the day. Traveling through the trees, two sifakas leap from one upright tree trunk to another. Traveling across the ground, two more sifakas hop sideways, their hands held above their heads, their movements jerky and awkward. In seconds the ring-tails and sifakas are face-to-face in a clearing.

A ring-tail squeaks. Another squawks. A young sifaka howls the call from which their name comes. SHI FAK! A juvenile ring-tailed lemur jumps at the noisy sifaka. Another sifaka leaps for a ring-tail.

But this is no battle. It is play. The ring-tailed lemurs and the sifakas roll and wrestle and leap about wildly. After a while, the sifakas seem to tire of the game and lope away as strangely as they came.

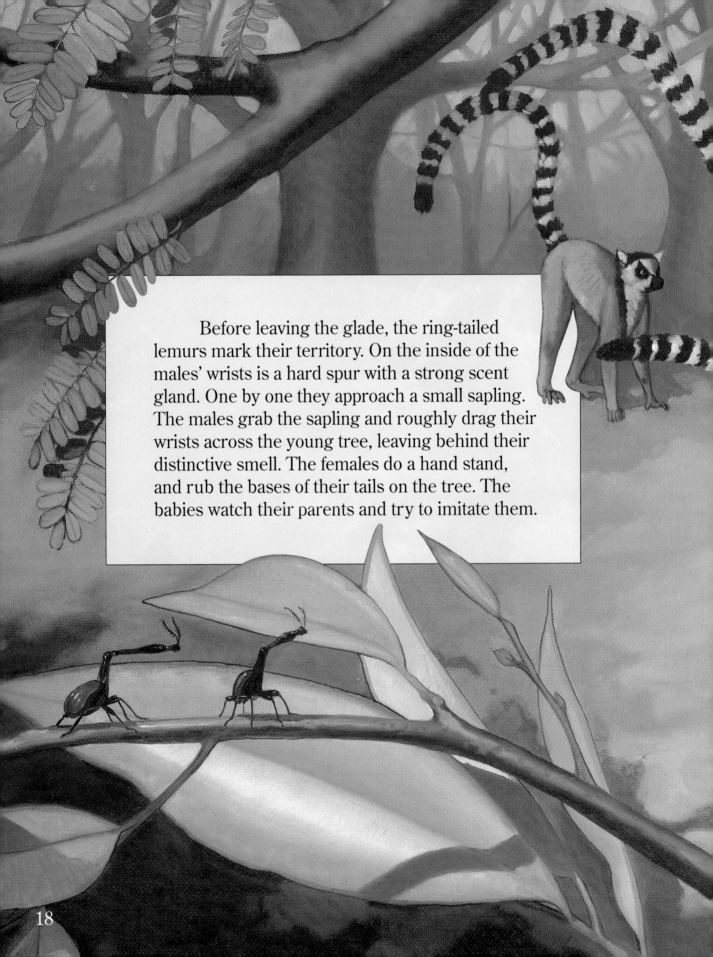

Before leaving the glade, the ring-tailed lemurs mark their territory. On the inside of the males' wrists is a hard spur with a strong scent gland. One by one they approach a small sapling. The males grab the sapling and roughly drag their wrists across the young tree, leaving behind their distinctive smell. The females do a hand stand, and rub the bases of their tails on the tree. The babies watch their parents and try to imitate them.

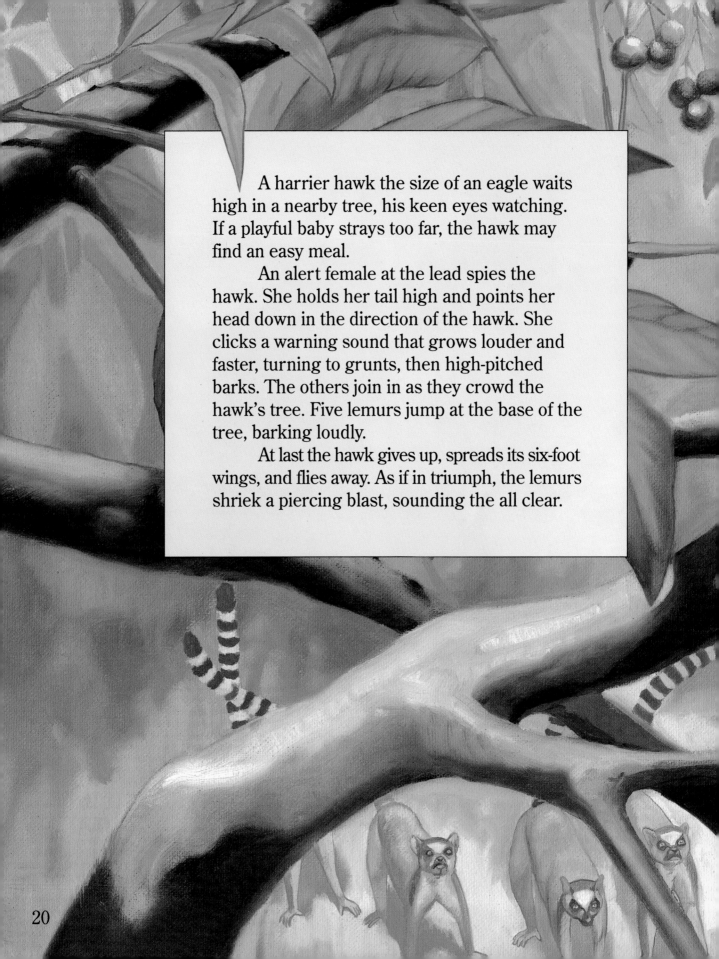

A harrier hawk the size of an eagle waits high in a nearby tree, his keen eyes watching. If a playful baby strays too far, the hawk may find an easy meal.

An alert female at the lead spies the hawk. She holds her tail high and points her head down in the direction of the hawk. She clicks a warning sound that grows louder and faster, turning to grunts, then high-pitched barks. The others join in as they crowd the hawk's tree. Five lemurs jump at the base of the tree, barking loudly.

At last the hawk gives up, spreads its six-foot wings, and flies away. As if in triumph, the lemurs shriek a piercing blast, sounding the all clear.

The next stop is a choice feeding area. But a neighboring troop of ring-tailed lemurs decides they too would like to feed here. It is time for a stink fight.

A newcomer moves to the front of his group. He sits on his haunches and rubs his wrist scent glands across scent glands on his upper chest. He grabs his tail and rubs it across his forearms. The lemur shakes his scented tail over his head in a high arc, sending waves of strong smell at the other lemurs.

Soon all of the males waft their scents as the females shriek and jump. When the stink fight is over, no one is injured. The neighboring troop has lost and must look for food elsewhere.

The lemurs feed hungrily on leaves, nuts, fruits and flowers in the clearing, then take their afternoon nap. When they awaken it is time to find a safe place for the night. Down the path they find one of their regular sleeping trees and easily run straight up the trunk of the giant tamarind. Crashing noisily about, they shriek and bark as they leap and cling from branch to branch. After a while they settle down, except for the baby who began the day so playfully.

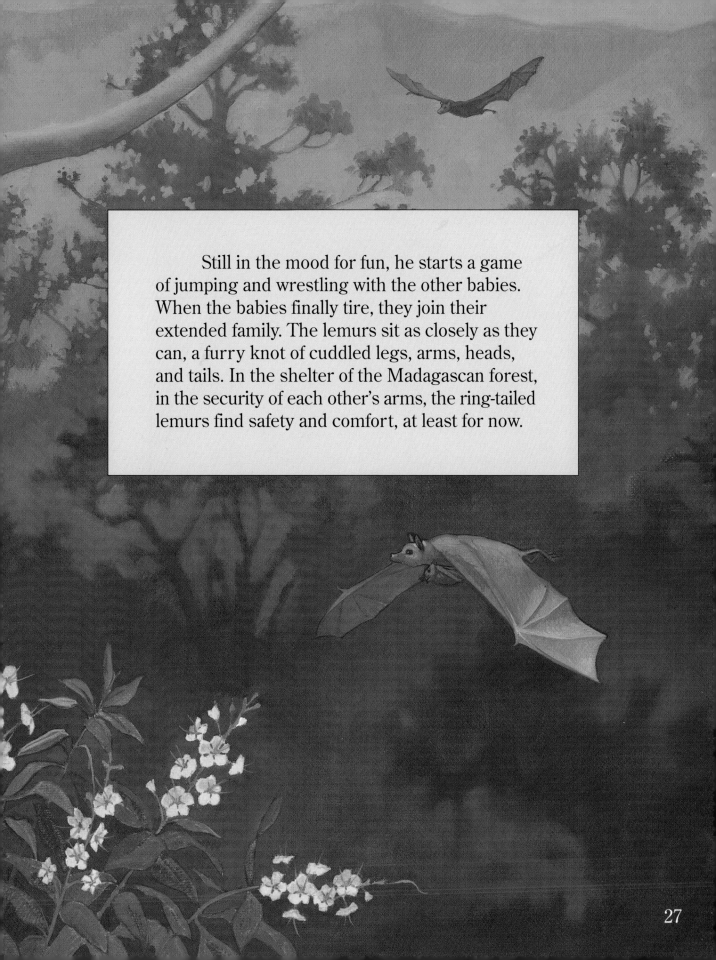

Still in the mood for fun, he starts a game of jumping and wrestling with the other babies. When the babies finally tire, they join their extended family. The lemurs sit as closely as they can, a furry knot of cuddled legs, arms, heads, and tails. In the shelter of the Madagascan forest, in the security of each other's arms, the ring-tailed lemurs find safety and comfort, at least for now.

Madagascar

Madagascar is an island 250 miles off the southeastern coast of Africa in the Indian Ocean. It is about 1,000 miles long and 350 miles at its widest point and is the fourth largest island in the world. Madagascar is home to rain forests in the east, 8,500 foot volcanic peaks surrounding a huge granite plateau in the center, and dry forests in the south and west.

About the Madagascan Tropical Dry Forest

Madagascar was once part of the continent of Africa, then it began to drift away to the east nearly 165 million years ago. This very slow movement of continents over time is called *continental drift*. Because Madagascar is so isolated 80 percent of plant and animal species in Madagascar live no where else in the world.

Tropical dry forests are just one of the fascinating and endangered habitats of Madagascar. These forests are tropical because they never freeze. They are dry because rainfall is scarce, only 30 inches each year. The rivers of southern Madagascar are fed with runoff rainwater from the central plateau. The trees in the dry forests depend on ground water from these rivers and from a brief rainy season. Tropical dry forest trees are smaller than trees in rain forests and drop their leaves for as long as six months of every year. Ring-tailed lemurs are found in these narrow green bands of forests along the rivers of the south.

Lemurs are prosimian primates. The word prosimian means before (pro) monkeys (simians). It is believed they look and act much like the ancestors of modern monkeys found in other parts of the world.

Like other primates, most lemurs have forward facing eyes and hands with opposable thumbs. Opposable thumbs are thumbs that can move across the palm of a hand to grasp and hold objects. Unlike other primates they do not have flat faces, but have dog-like muzzles. They are small, ranging from mouse-sized to cat-sized. Ring-tailed lemurs weigh only about 6 pounds. Their bottom front teeth are flattened, grooved and used for grooming.

When people first arrived in Madagascar less than 2,000 years ago, there were nearly 50 species of lemur, including one as big as a gorilla. Today there are only about 30 species of lemur left. Many of those are endangered. All of them are threatened because their habitats or homes are threatened. To protect the lemurs, the tropical dry forests where they live must be saved.

Glossary

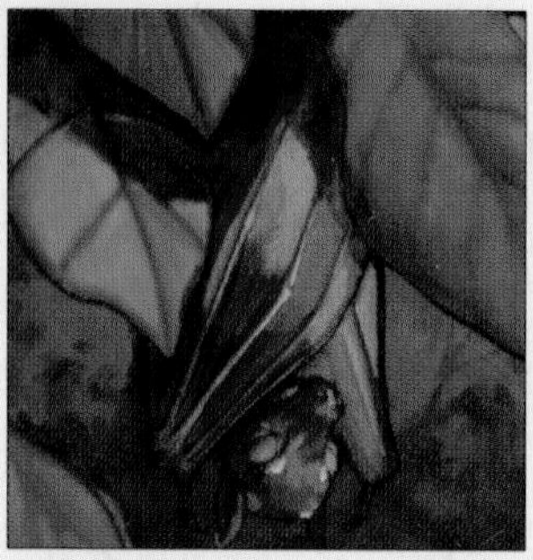

▲ *Flying fox*

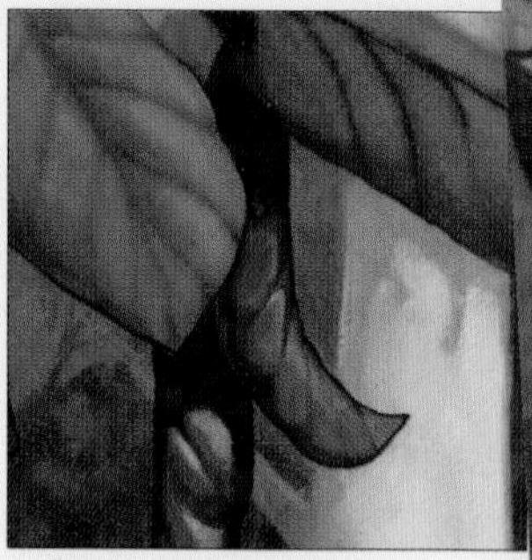

▲ *Baikiaea bean*

▲ *Acridocarpa natalus*

▲ *Hoopoe*

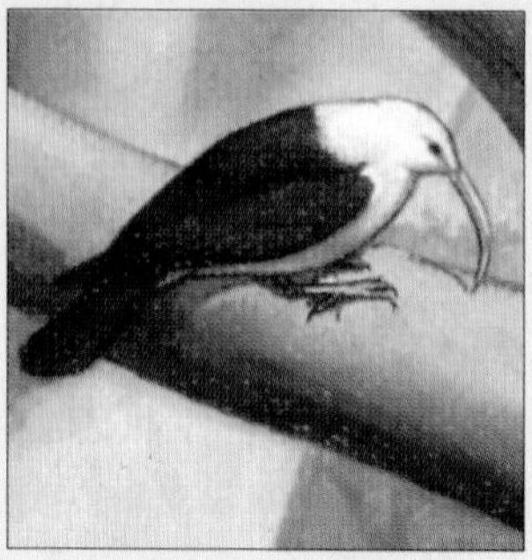

▲ *Sickle-billed vanga*

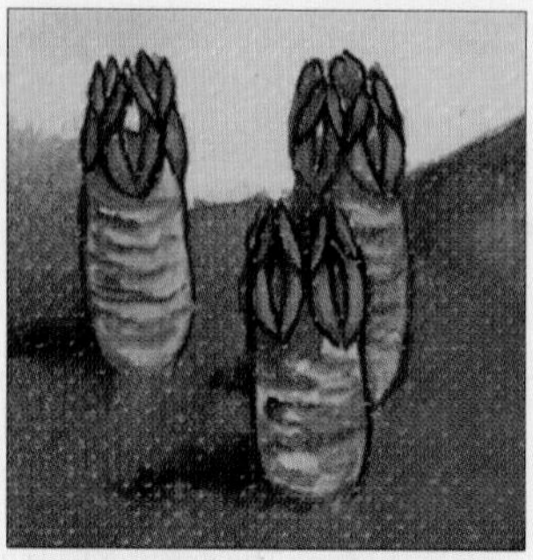

▲ *Rafflesia*

▲ *Giant coua*

▲ *Madagascar paradise flycatcher*

▲ *R*

▲ ...y

▲ Sifaka

▲ Madagascar harrier-hawk

▲ ...mur

▲ Giraffe weevil

▲ Parson's chameleon

▲ ...r cicada

▲ Tamarind tree

▲ Tamarind